D1083627

JAPANESE GROTESQUERIES

JAPANESE GROTESQUERIES

compiled by Nikolas Kiej'e

with an introductory essay

by Terence Barrow, Ph.D.

CHARLES E. TUTTLE COMPANY

Rutland, Vermont & Tokyo, Japan

REPRESENTATIVES

For Continental Europe:
BOXERBOOKS, INC., *Zurich*

For the British Isles:
PRENTICE-HALL INTERNATIONAL, INC., *London*

For Australasia:
PAUL FLESCH & CO., PTY. LTD., *Melbourne*

For Canada:
M. G. HURTIG, LTD., *Edmonton*

Published by the Charles E. Tuttle Company, Inc.
of Rutland, Vermont & Tokyo, Japan
with editorial offices at
Suido 1-chome, 2–6, Bunkyo-ku, Tokyo

Library of Congress Catalog Card No. 73–75283
International Standard Book No. 0–8048 0656–x

First printing, 1973

PRINTED IN JAPAN

TABLE OF CONTENTS

Ghosts, Ghost-Gods, & Demons of Japan
by Terence Barrow, Ph.D. — *page* 7

ILLUSTRATIONS

I Female Ghosts (*Figures 1–18*) 29
II Suicide, Monsters, & Freaks (*Figures 19–97*) 61
III Ghouls & Skeletons (*Figures 98–109*) 169
IV Murder (*Figures 110–117*) 189
V Hells & Demons (*Figures 118–123*) 205
VI Magical Animals (*Figures 124–141*) 219
VII Fabulous Creatures (*Figures 142–155*) 245

GHOSTS, GHOST-GODS, & DEMONS OF JAPAN

by Terence Barrow, Ph.D.

JAPANESE GHOSTS, GHOST-GODS, AND DEMONS APPEAR IN the traditional art and literature in an abundance unequaled in any other culture. They are of diverse kinds, both good and evil. Some are of enormous horror and not a little humor. Throughout the centuries the Japanese people have enjoyed exotic and fantastic things—ghost stories and ghost pictures being high on the list of entertainment and pleasure available to the common man. "Ghost evenings" in private homes were once much in vogue. Eerie stories brought the primordial thrill of creeping flesh and tingling spine that civilized man enjoys. Even the thought of a walk home alone through darkened streets did not deter those with a taste for ghost evenings with their friends. Today not many people in East or West will admit to belief in ghosts, yet after dark only one person in a hundred will willingly cross a graveyard alone.

Japanese traditions of the supernatural depicted in literature and art combine Chinese ideas of demons, Indian notions of the transmigration of souls, and the native Shinto belief in nature and animal spirits. This merging has yielded a rich assortment of grotesque creatures, all of them odd, bizarre, and contrary to human notions of what is normal. The horror of some of these supernatural creatures, such as baby-eating ghouls and cannibalistic monsters, is relieved only by the underlying sense of humor which is a persistent trait of the Japanese character. Without it the subjects, especially as portrayed in pictures, would be horrid and sordid.

Most of the illustrations which this essay introduces are derived from the Edo period (1615–1867) or from the early part of the Meiji era, which commenced in 1868. In Edo times art and literature produced such an abundance of grotesque and frightful creatures that administrators realized that the public mind was becoming infected by a kind of fever. In 1808 the government legislated against ghost stories which featured flying heads, animal goblins, serpent monsters, fire demons, and accounts of the atrocities or manners of vicious women.

In 1808 the ordinary Japanese believed that ghosts, ghost-gods, ghouls, and demons actually existed. As in other countries living at the folk level of culture, the Japanese in the eras before the Meiji Restoration lived out their daily lives affected by hundreds of superstitions. One was that to the northeast lay the Ura-kimon, literally "back-door," meaning Demon's Gate. From that direction came demons and misfortune, so no doors were built facing that way, no matter how pleasant the aspect.

The change of attitudes away from superstition is especially evident in the wide use of cameras in Japan today. No people have more cameras, yet the old-fashioned folk of earlier Japan believed a camera to be dangerous to the soul of the sitter. In 1840 when Lord Narioka of Nagasaki secured an old daguerreotype camera, the retainer chosen to act as subject committed suicide rather than run the risk of having his soul sucked from his body. Narioka's son bravely came forward to have taken what is perhaps Japan's first photographic portrait.

Most Japanese ghost stories can be identified as coming from one of two distinct sources. The ghosts and other supernatural creatures of earliest origin come from the pre-Buddhist period. This was the Age of the Gods, when early Shinto teachings held that the natural world was at one with the supernatural world and that spirits inhabited birds and beasts, trees, rocks, natural phenomena, and even artifacts. In those days all things were alive in their own way and had the power to speak. Although composed after the advent of Buddhism, the eighth-century chronicles of the *Kojiki* and the *Nihon Shoki*, or *Nihongi,* contain supernatural tales from the pre-Buddhist period. Ghosts first make their appearance in the *Kojiki.*

It was the coming of Buddhism to Japan via the Korean peninsula about A.D. 552 that inaugurated the second or the post-Buddhist phase of ghost stories. Classic Japanese art, in which grotesqueries have such an important place, thrives in this second period. Later, in the Edo period, the toggles called *netsuke* were also especially rich in the grotesqueries. It is in this second phase that Chinese ghost stories and Buddhist ideas of hells make such an impact on the Japanese imagination. The old childlike simplicity of the Age of the Gods of Shinto is made complex by foreign intrusions.

From the advent of Buddhism to the beginning of the Meiji era the old stories from India and China were combined with indigenous tales. One can also detect elements shared with cultures in Polynesia and Southeast Asia; the mythology and collection of spiritual beings of these areas have much in common. However, it is the changing fashions in Japanese ghosts that are most likely to attract the attention of students of ghosts in Japanese tradition. Ghosts of the Muromachi period (1393–1573) are at first rich in goblins and ogres, to be replaced later with more poetic, romantic, and even sexually inclined ghosts. In Edo times ghosts assumed sensational roles, but at the same time the monsters seem to become more sympathetic to human beings, the demons more considerate.

The greatest master of Japanese grotesqueries is Katsushika Hokusai (1760–1849). Over his long life he made thousands of sketches, mostly for woodblocks. His famous fifteen-volume collection of drawings known as the *Hokusai Manga* (Hokusai's Ten Thousand Sketches) is a monumental work rich in grotesqueries. An admirable selection with comment was made by James A. Michener in *The Hokusai Sketchbooks*. In this book Michener coined the term "grotesqueries" for this particular genre of Japanese art. In fact Michener was one of the first scholars to give this aspect of Japanese art the attention it deserves. Grotesqueries have appeared to the Western eye as Oriental eccentricities; yet they are a meaningful and symbolic expression of Japanese art and literature.

Foreign scholars working in Japan have often been fascinated by Japanese grotesqueries. Chief among them is Lafcadio Hearn (1850–1905), who, after moving to Japan in 1891, married a Japanese woman and absorbed himself in the deepest of Japanese traditions. His books *Kwaidan, Stories and Studies of Strange Things, Shadowings, In Ghostly Japan, Exotics and Retrospectives,* and *Kokoro: Hints and Echoes of Japanese Inner Life* are rich in tales and thoughts about the supernatural in Japan. In one of Hearn's stories (appearing in *In Ghostly Japan*), a Tengu, out of gratitude to a priest who had saved his life, allowed the priest to have his heart's desire—to be present as the Lord Buddha gave his sermon on Vulture Peak. Unfortunately the priest broke his promise to keep his eyes closed during the sermon, so his ravishing experience was abruptly ended. He was a disconsolate priest thereafter. Impossible as this story may sound, science is seriously considering the prospects of man's going back in time to former events of history, time being quite elastic.

The Western world has its own rich tradition of ghosts and grotesqueries, expecially from ages before the Renaissance, when the European mind was poetic rather than technological. The art, literature, and folklore of the Celtic and Germanic peoples of Europe are a storehouse of dragons, goblins, heroic gods, trolls, sprites, elves, giants, wizards, magical swords, and superhuman beings who confront the powers of evil. Viking art, early English and French illuminated manuscripts, and the stone and wood carving of Gothic churches all exhibit a remarkable range of grotesqueries. The nightmarish oils of the Flemish painter Hieronymus Bosch, with their hells, devils, monsters, and semihuman freaks, belong to the fevered imagination of the medieval age, when men avidly believed in wizards, witches, walking dead, monsters, and devils. Peter Bruegel the Elder, who succeeded Bosch, carried on the European tradition of grotesqueries, just as did the twentieth-century surrealist painter Salvador Dali.

Traditional Japanese grotesqueries rarely served to teach a moral, as did the medieval European. Other than when using images of Buddhist hells to stress what fate the wicked can expect, Japanese ghosts are usually amoral, or bent on vengeance or plain mischief. On the other hand, Western ghosts and freaks of the afterworld are based on human prototypes, and however much they moan or rattle chains, they rarely harm people. (The vampire is an exception, but that image is based on folklore of the bat. A significant truth is that bloodsucking bats have a high incidence of rabies, which brings frenzied madness to any human infected. This fact is probably at the root of vampire tales.)

If we are to find a rival to Japanese imagination in grotesqueries we must turn to the traditions of India, Tibet, and China. Tibet is especially rich in supernatural grotesqueries, but in general Japanese artists surpass all others. Their demons, ghouls, ogres, devils, magical animals, he-ghosts and she-ghosts, gods, and spirits of nature have a special "flavor." They are humorous and terrible at the same time, just as the typical Japanese mind is inclined to both humor and the morbid. What other culture has created voyeuristic ghosts, which are among the most delightful of supernatural creatures, or such an army of ghouls?

Japanese ghosts and spiritual beings fall into various classes. Each kind has its particular environment and personal habits. For example, the Shinto-derived Tengu has such distinctive appearance and habitat that it is not likely to be confused with a Buddhist Oni.

Broadly speaking, supernatural creatures fit into one or another of the following classes: 1) spirits of dead persons, usually resentful and full of envy for the living, of which the spirits of stillborn children and frustrated women are the most dangerous; 2) nature spirits that can enter things or animals, which then take on a magical form; 3) the spirits of inanimate nature, such as are found in trees, plants, or stones; 4) man-made artifacts which walk and talk, such as utensils, tools, pots, bridges, or walls; 5) natural phenomena, such as air, fire, and water spirits; 6) subhuman or supernatural children conceived in sexual unions with humans by gods, demons, magical animals, and such supernatural beings; 6) animals transformed into humans. These groups provide the subject matter of Japanese grotesqueries.

The "physical" appearance of ghosts or spirits of the various types is diverse. Ghosts of dead persons can be invisible, but if they appear they may be identified by silver patches seen where the eyebrows should be, and the legs are usually missing. The tradition of legless ghosts is relatively late in the history of Japanese ghosts. In an old story a couple of girl ghosts clatter along wearing wooden clogs. Legless ghosts were especially popular in Edo times—that was the fashionable ghost of the day. Another characteristic of ghosts is that their bodies tend to taper to a narrow wavering end and cast no shadow. (It is an old tradition in Japan that as death nears, the human shadow grows less sharply defined.) Ghosts' features are haggard and pale, and their hair falls loosely over face and shoulders. Hands are raised to the breast, leaving the fingers drooping downwards. Ghostly clothing is usually white.

Living skeletons are common in the Japanese tradition, but far less favored than in the Western ghost stories. Curious forms of ghosts relate to particular stories. For example, there is a female ghost with two mouths fed by her long hair, which terminates in hands. Such a frightening daughter is said to be born to parents who are stingy with a stepdaughter to the point of starving her to death.

Females with no eyes, or one eye, or a wavering head extending out from the body on a snakelike neck, are among the most terrifying of ghosts. The Japanese agree that female ghosts are as unrelenting as the blade of a steel sword. They are dreaded by living men, their wives, and paramours, as a deceased wife with a grudge can return to haunt the living and drive them to distraction, suicide, or murder, in the mad frenzy of fear that the apparition inspires.

The Japanese believe that ghosts, monsters, goblins, freaks, and other undesirable spirits can be exorcised with priestly help. Oriental evil spirits abhor and run from sacred Buddhist sutras or chanted prayers, just as evil ghosts in Christian countries traditionally are put to flight before a crucifix or a Bible. Salt cast at ghosts is also effective in driving them off, while images or talismanic objects at entrances prevent ghosts from getting into a house or a temple.

In modern times Shinto and Buddhist ceremonies are available for the exorcism of undesirable spirits, as indeed there are such ceremonies in certain Christian churches of America and Europe. From time to time newspapers throughout the world report that haunting ghosts have appeared in one place or another, with descriptions of acts done to oust the ghost. Serious ghost-hunter reports are so convincing that one should keep an open mind on the subject. In the older traditions the supernatural forces take on the form of demons and other stereotyped forms, but spiritual forces of the kind investigated scientifically are more kinetic, ectoplasmic, audible, and irrational.

In Japan, in early February, *setsubun* marks the end of winter, and by tradition it is the time to scatter roast beans before the house and dispel with added shouts any loitering evil spirits. Another custom, not much followed today, is to hang the head of a dead fish on holly at the household door. This is said to drive away evil spirits by the distasteful odor of the fish, while insects retreat before the prickly holly.

Generally speaking, the near-supernatural world has always been distrusted. The gods on high are far away, but the spirits of the dead and unseen beings intent on evil wander about the habitations of men. For this reason sculptures of fierce aspect, representing the great Indian gods Indra and Brahma, often stand before many Buddhist temples. Common houses may have roof-end tiles with demon faces serving as protective emblems, a custom now out of vogue but still to be seen. Ghosts are reputed to hold a senseless animosity to living men, and it is only by magical devices or quick wit that human beings can survive their malignancy.

An example of lack of discrimination on the part of ghosts and of human skill in turning the tables is found in one tale: An innocent traveler, while crossing a haunted bridge of old Japan, met a woman who asked him to deliver a letter she was carrying to someone waiting on another bridge. The man courteously complied but later checked the letter, which read, "Kill the bearer." To safeguard himself he rewrote the message as "Do not kill the bearer." When he delivered the letter to a fierce-looking ghost at the other bridge, this second ghost was nonplused and allowed the man to escape unharmed.

The traditional rule is, if you meet a ghost, run away. The grateful dead are rare in ghost stories; however, a few are to be found. A man passing a bamboo grove heard a voice wailing: "Oh, how my eyes hurt! Oh, how my eyes hurt!" Being overcome with curiosity, he went into the gloomy grove and there found a skeleton with bamboos growing through the eyes of its skull. Out of sympathy for the tortured spirit he removed the bamboo shoots and was later thanked by the ghost of the dead man. However, ghosts are unpredictable, and he might have been murdered for his kindness.

At the level of daily life in old Japan the ghosts of dead women were most dreaded. Horrible to behold, these female spirits were both malicious and revengeful, with or without reason. Nothing could placate them except the death of an unfaithful lover or husband, and often a current mistress of the man suffered, too. A complicating feature of female ghosts was their disturbing ability to deceive living men into marrying them by appearing as normal and beautiful women. Among the most terrible of female spirits was the Yuki Onna, or Snow Woman, of ghastly visage, who appeared in snowstorms to cause travelers to fall asleep in their tracks, there to freeze to death. No doubt this superstition developed from the sleeping deaths that come to anyone fatigued and exposed to extreme cold. The Hannya is a female demon child-eater, well known from her appearances in the Noh drama. Kabuki and Noh stage plays are rich in ghostly characters, and the Japanese consider the portrayal of them a true test of the actor's art.

We may now consider particular supernatural beings of Japanese tradition. Oni spirits are thought to be a direct import from China. They eat and drink like human beings, have a devilish temper, are often of gigantic size, and in color are gray, red, pink, or blue. They usually have horns, three toes, three fingers, and three eyes—in all, rather frightening for a man to meet. Oni are as unintelligent as they are undesirable. Malicious, cruel, and lecherous with their human victims, it is hard to find any saving grace in Oni.

Tengu, on the other hand, are spirits ranked as minor deities of ancient Shinto origin. They favor habitation on the cryptomeria groves set about temples, or they may live in the mountains. Tengu resemble the Garuda of India and Southeast Asia, and like the Garuda they are bird-man messengers of the gods. Their form is variable, but they are commonly winged. Their noses look like bird beaks. Appropriately, they like to wear red cloaks covered with feathers or leaves. On their heads they often wear small black hats. By their nature Tengu are not as intent on evil as on mischief, although they occasionally kill human beings who play tricks on them. Expert swordsmen, they have been known to impart this art to men whom for some reason or other they have come to favor.

Kappa are water imps, perhaps the most fascinating of Japan's many supernatural creatures. They are, from a human point of view, completely unpredictable, as they are both benevolent and malevolent. If people do some deed favorable to them, or if they are rightly placated, they may make good servants who can impart to mortals such useful and difficult arts as bonesetting.

The facial features of Kappa resemble those of monkeys, from whom they are said to have descended. As messengers of the river god Kappa, they are primarily associated with the waters of ponds, rivers, lakes, and streams. Curiously, some have tortoise shells on their backs. In color they are yellow-green, while in size they are no bigger than a child. Their small size does not indicate harmlessness, however. They are notorious drinkers of human blood and singularly tricky in their behavior. They are dangerous to humans who cannot resist a challenge. They enjoy "pull-finger," preferably at the water's edge, where they can drag in the human opponent so he will drown before they drink his blood. Adult or child, it is all the same to Kappa. They enter the body of a victim via the anus. When drowned men, women, or children are found with a bulging of the anus (a symptom of death by drowning) the country folk say it must be the work of a Kappa and cite the evidence.

In spite of their vicious nature Kappa are comical favorites rather misrepresented in Edo times as lovable imps. They commonly keep their promises to human beings, but, like Oni, they are rapists and lechers. R. H. Blyth, the most sympathetic of Westerners ever to comment on Japanese culture, tells the story of a lecherous Kappa in his fascinating *Oriental Humor*. In this tale the wife of a samurai went to a temple and was there greeted by a beautiful boy, who she thought was an acolyte. This pretty young woman was startled when this boy, whom she believed to be intent on religion, started to wink at her, then tried to hold her hand. Indignantly the woman left the temple before making her usual offering of incense at the altar. He followed her home. That evening this young fellow, who in reality was a Kappa, hid under the lavatory in the house and at first opportunity touched the woman's private parts. In sudden anger the woman cut off the arm of the Kappa, who later came to her to plead for its return.

The weakness of Kappa is a curious hollow on the crown of their heads. It is filled with a fluid, the spilling of which causes them temporary loss of strength. As Kappa like to wrestle, any person encountering one is advised to make a challenge, then bow deeply. The Kappa will, through courtesy, return the bow, causing the liquid to flow out of the crown cup, thus weakening him and allowing the person time to escape. In a wrestling bout with a Kappa the human being should do his best to spill the liquid. Kappa have a liking for cucumbers; so another means of effecting a foil is to throw cucumbers in their direction to divert their attention long enough to make an escape.

Japanese demons serve in many capacities, especially as servants in hell, where their task is to torment the souls of the dead for their sins on earth. Demons serve the gods, act as guardians of temples, and may become servants of man if they are bettered in a contest. They change their form at will and generally frequent bamboo groves, gateways, toilets, bathhouses, and ordinary dwellings. By nature they are soft-hearted and benevolent to the virtuous, but the evil they taunt and torment in life as they do spirits in hell. Demons are strong, ugly, given to bouts of foul temper, and are generally regarded as intellectually stupid. They enjoy wrestling with their own kind or with human beings. However, it is generally held that only saints or superhuman heroes are capable of overcoming or driving away the most powerful of demons.

To the traditional Japanese of post-Buddhist ages, hell or Hades was a grim reality. The thought of hell haunted him just as it did the mind of medieval man. In a kind of Japanese All Saints' Day, or Hallowe'en, Emma-sama, the Lord of Hades, supposedly released from *jigoku*, or hell, the tormented spirits in a brief respite so that they could annually visit their former homes. For this reason the terrible Emma-sama has temples and is prayed to by many. The Japanese hells surpass in horror the hell of Dante's *Inferno,* even as hell was portrayed in the engravings of Gustav Doré. The hell of old Japan was set under the sea. Even children had their special hell, named Hariyama, or Needle Mountain.

The spirit world of Japanese tradition, which provides the raw material for grotesqueries in art and literature, included magical animals. A variety of freaks and monsters of animal kind were usually the product of the unnatural sexual unions of human beings with foxes, badger, cats, and other magical animals. Freaks are especially feared because they lack saving graces; they are best avoided or placated by any means possible.

Of magical animals the white fox is king of beasts, for it is messenger to the gods. The rice god Inari has as his earthly symbol the white fox. Women were often possessed by the spirits of foxes which, in human form, mixed among humans and sometimes married. Regardless of outward appearance, the shadow of a fox-woman is always that of a fox. A beautiful woman casting a fox shadow is a favorite theme in Japanese art. Fox-women produced children that appeared human, and they were often devoted mothers and wives. However, return to their own kind was inevitable, and many sad partings are depicted.

Weasels and martens were also capable of assuming human form except for their tail parts, which remained unchanged. This feature often alerted human acquaintances to their true nature. Badgers also joined the ranks of man-imitators by transforming themselves into human beings. One of the tricks of badgers was to lure young ladies out at night by playing on drums. Then, when they were far from their houses, the lustful badgers seduced them. Western ghosts and magical creatures seem singularly uninterested in sex, but in contrast many of the Japanese supernatural animals or other spirits are inclined to make love, marry, be voyeuristic, or be lustful to the point of rape of human women.

Like the witches' cats of Europe, magical cats were feared by Japanese above all the magical animals because of their sinister qualities. A folk belief in Japan holds that old cats learn to understand human speech, and for this reason cats were, in times past, seldom kept into their old age. It is well known that mortal cats are able to remember any evil done them by humans, and in folklore this real trait of living cats has become an attribute of supernatural cats. A curious folk custom of old Japan was to break the tails of cats because of a belief that they had the power to dance on their tails in order to make someone die. The common saying regarding these broken tails, however, was that they had been stepped on by demons.

Among magical animals badgers are regarded as the temperamental tricksters. They are amenable to kindness but at heart are malicious. Fortunately they are foolish enough to be easily bemused. Badgers have the curious ability to turn themselves into inanimate objects. One tale relates how a badger converted itself into a teakettle for the convenience of a Buddhist priest who had saved its life.

Another magical animal of Japan, the marten, has a minor role as a supernatural creature. Superstition has it that the sight of a marten in any place indicates there is a ghost nearby. The hare, like the monkey and the toad, is treated as a comical creature who engages in human acts and frolickings. Hare stories are very old in Japan.

As in the fables of the Greek slave Aesop, supernatural animals mimic men, talk like human beings, and walk on their hind legs, while engaging in all kinds of mischief. Artists often use them to satirize human failings and foibles, an excellent example of this being the famous twelfth-century *Choju Giga* scroll, in which monkeys, hares, and frogs grapple, race, sit in contemplation, or argue with one another. The belief that men could turn into animals is in accord with the Buddhist teaching of reincarnation, which holds that human beings transmigrate through various bodies. Regardless of the serious side of supernatural things, the saving grace of humor is always with us in Japanese grotesqueries. Artists and craftsmen aimed at frightening and amusing simultaneously.

Cocks have a special place in the symbolism of Shinto religion as birds of the gods; however, they rarely appear in ghost stories. One amusing tale in the *Yokai Kidan* relates how a certain hypocritical monk stole a cock to secretly cook for a private feast. The bird's owner learned of the circumstances and charged the priest with theft, only to get the reply that as monks were virtuous and devoted to austerity, how could he, a monk, do such a terrible thing? At the moment he finished speaking, a loud "Cock-a-doodle-doo" issued from his mouth, and he took on the appearance of a cock. The priest was obliged to admit his guilt.

Fabulous animals include the dragon-horse or *kirin*, best known today as the brand label of a popular beer. Like the Chinese dragon, the *kirin* whirls along on flames and clouds. Some dogs also possess supernatural powers to make appearances as magical animals. There is one notorious dog that follows travelers and can only be deterred if the traveler pelts him with rice balls or lies down and proclaims that he is too tired to go on.

Insects also appear as supernatural creatures, often in monstrous form. They are even capable of expressing gratitude when aided by human beings. One story relates that a bee, released from a spider's web by a samurai, later turned the samurai's near defeat into victory by bringing a swarm of companion bees to put the man's opponent to flight. Crabs, too, have a place in the supernatural world. Certain kinds are identified as the spirits of defeated Taira clan warriors whose restless forms can be seen in crab or human form, haunting the rocks and waters. Some animals were thought to hold natural enmities for other species, an example being the crab and monkey, which can never agree on anything.

The miscellaneous ghosts of Japan are those that are of individual types which do not readily fit into one large category either in appearance or behavior. One of these unusual supernatural creatures is the *nopperabo*, which looks like a jelly blob resembling the head of a man with arms and legs attached. Another odd ghost, called *kinaki jiji*, is an old man whose apparition weeps like a child to evoke sympathy from those who pass by. However, if anyone stops to comfort him he clings to him as tenaciously as the troublesome old man who climbed on the back of Sinbad the Sailor.

The most unusual Japanese ghosts are supernatural beings in the form of natural forces or elements. A striking example of such a ghost in Japanese history concerns the great Hideyoshi Toyotomi, who in the sixteenth century rose from common birth to become the most powerful man in all Japan. His rise to fame and power is said to have been gained from the favor of a thunder spirit. Apparently Hideyoshi had released it after it had become wedged in the branches of a nettle tree.

Skeletons and skulls are the stock-in-trade of the Japanese writer and artist, just as they are in Western ghost stories or pictures. In Japan they have a stronger power as symbols of death. The very sight of a skeleton brought chills to the heart of even a dauntless samurai. The appearance of skulls anywhere suggests the presence of malignant spirits. The impact on the Japanese imagination is greater because the skull is regarded as more than a mere symbol of death.

The plates that follow illustrate most of the ghosts and magical animals mentioned above. These illustrations represent a tradition that was very much alive and believed in a hundred years ago. The people for whom these plates were made, and the writers who used them as illustrations, actually believed such things were possible. Some were skeptical, and a few were outright disbelievers, but the majority of early Meiji, Edo, and pre-Edo Japanese did believe implicitly in ghosts and supernatural creatures of all kinds.

Today, we ask, do ghosts live? Do ghosts die? Some very intelligent people believe that ghosts are mental projections that form apparitions which, by the power of thought transference, can be seen by several people at one time without having any substantial reality. Others believe in ghosts, pure and simple. Spiritualists of modern times claim that they can speak with the dead of recent and past ages; however, there never has been any scientific proof of this.

The simple fact remains that throughout recorded history people have claimed to have seen and heard ghosts. At the primitive level of culture, through which all nations have passed, ghosts and ghost-gods dominated daily existence, and no important domestic or social act was done without consulting them. Every anthropologist knows that ghosts are abundant in folk cultures and are generally feared by mankind.

Modern man appears to see ghosts with less and less frequency as fear of his living neighbors becomes his preoccupation. Electric light has done much to dispel ghost beliefs. Changes in the environment due to concrete apartments, television, radio, and telephones, as well as the noise of automobiles and jet aircraft, have had a deadening effect on the psychic life by which man lived in past ages.

Advances in science have a numbing effect on man's poetic and deepest consciousness. Who could have imagined a century ago, least of all in Japan, that man would soon be watching moving pictures, speaking to persons on the other side of the world, walking on the moon, or making weapons that could obliterate cities in an instant?

The wonders of the twentieth century outdo anything that Japanese grotesqueries can offer, but charm is lacking in the modern marvels. Perhaps that is why there is a need for a book such as this. We seek a return to the world of human imagination and to the deep unconscious by which our most distant ancestors lived. The conscious mind of man is merely a surface reflection of the deep subconscious with its ancient hopes and primitive fears. It is in this uncharted realm of the mind, of dreams and intuitions, that artists and writers find the images of their art. Japanese grotesqueries, an inheritance to the world of one aspect of a great culture, should do much to amuse us, to bestir our imaginations, and to better let us understand traditional Japan.

PART I

FEMALE GHOSTS

30 JAPANESE GROTESQUERIES: FEMALE GHOSTS

§1. Japan's most feared ghost is Oiwa, the ghost of vengeance in the famous ghost story *Yotsuya Kaidan*. In an effort to escape from Oiwa, her husband hides in an old abandoned house. The single paper lantern he has used for light begins to take the shape of his wife's face, and her body is seen in the ivy vines. A beaded curtain supernaturally takes the shape of snakes, and some vines also become animate in the form of snakes.

小倉
擬百人一首
大中臣能宣朝臣

32 JAPANESE GROTESQUERIES: FEMALE GHOSTS

§2. Seldom are the wicked so well punished as they are in Japan. This moral concept has a strong Western flavor foreign to most traditional Japanese ideas. A feudal lord begins to taste future torments while visited by ghosts and demons. A folding screen depicting a landscape begins to take on the appearance of weird skulls, while the grotesque outlines of a woman whom he has murdered also emerge from the scene. A demonic hand of a monster reaches to caress him, and before him a ghostly shape begins to materialize.

細久手
堀越
大領

34 JAPANESE GROTESQUERIES: FEMALE GHOSTS

§3. A puppeteer who has constantly manipulated dolls in a famous play concerning a murdered woman's ghost and her lover is himself helplessly trapped in a ghostly re-enactment of the story. Tampering with the past fate of the dead is never a healthy idea, for there is sympathetic magic in such acts.

36 JAPANESE GROTESQUERIES: FEMALE GHOSTS

§4. In the West, summoning a ghost is a lengthy and somewhat complicated process. This is not the case in the East. Eastern ghosts are most obliging and will appear to human beings. Here an artist, all too skillful, is shocked out of his senses by having his ghost painting suddenly come alive.

芳年随筆
応挙之幽霊

§5. Oiwa returns to her husband in the form of a long-tailed ghost. Hidden behind the screen is her husband's new lover, Matsue, who does not know that the woman with him is his dead wife. Thus a chain of jealousy is forged.

尾上

40 JAPANESE GROTESQUERIES: FEMALE GHOSTS

§6. Not even Buddhist priests are safe from ghostly apparitions. While on the old Tokaido road, coming from Osaka to Tokyo, the priest Yuten is visited by a ghost who attempts to sway him to commit an evil act by exerting her powerful influence. Grasping his prayer beads, the priest resists the ghost and foils her designs on him.

累の怨魂
祐天和尚

42 JAPANESE GROTESQUERIES: FEMALE GHOSTS

§7. The ghost Oiwa makes her grim appearance before a mortal man, quite terrifying him with her ghastly visage. Between them the shadowy figure of a man holding a teapot makes its strange manifestation.

§8. A gentle woman during her life, Oiwa returns to her faithless husband in the shape of a horrible and mutilated woman. By her visitations she frightens him into remorse, repentance, and finally to insanity and death.

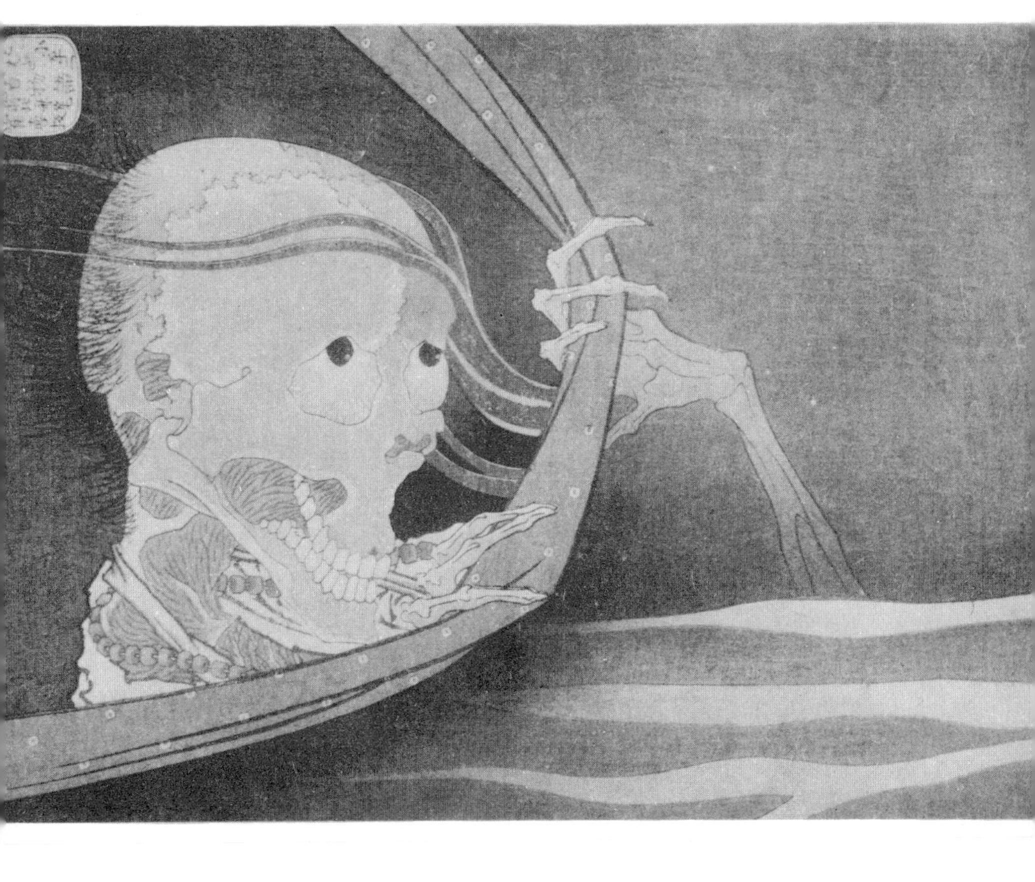

§9. The gaiety of an engagement party is destroyed by Oiwa's visit to her husband. Frightened out of his wits, he unsheathes his sword and, trembling with fear, slashes at the ghost of his dead wife. His second bride-to-be and the guests are astonished at his action, for they cannot see or hear the ghost. The first seeds of doubt as to the ill-fated man's sanity are planted among his friends.

§10. Terrified at the apparition of his dead wife, the husband of Oiwa attempts to drive her away by slashing at her with his sword. But swords have no effect on ghosts, and Oiwa's revenge will not be denied.

神谷伊右ヱ門
一勇斎國芳画

50 JAPANESE GROTESQUERIES: FEMALE GHOSTS

§11. From the depths of a well, the quavering voice of a young girl is heard counting slowly, "One . . . two . . . three . . ." It is the ghost of Saucer Mansion, who is doomed to count eternally, as she did in life, the number of saucers her father owned. Because she had broken one of a priceless collection, her father had her bound and thrown into a well as punishment. On moonless nights the ghost of the young girl returns to the top of the well, and with ghostly voice she resumes her never-ending tally.

§12. This Oiwa of deathly aspect wanders through the night, with outstretched arms and bony hands. White robes and loose, flowing hair are typical of Oiwa.

§13. A softened candle in a paper lantern falls on its side and gutters. The candle's flame licks at the frail material, and the lantern begins to burn slowly and assumes the visage of the ghost of the mutilated and murdered Oiwa.

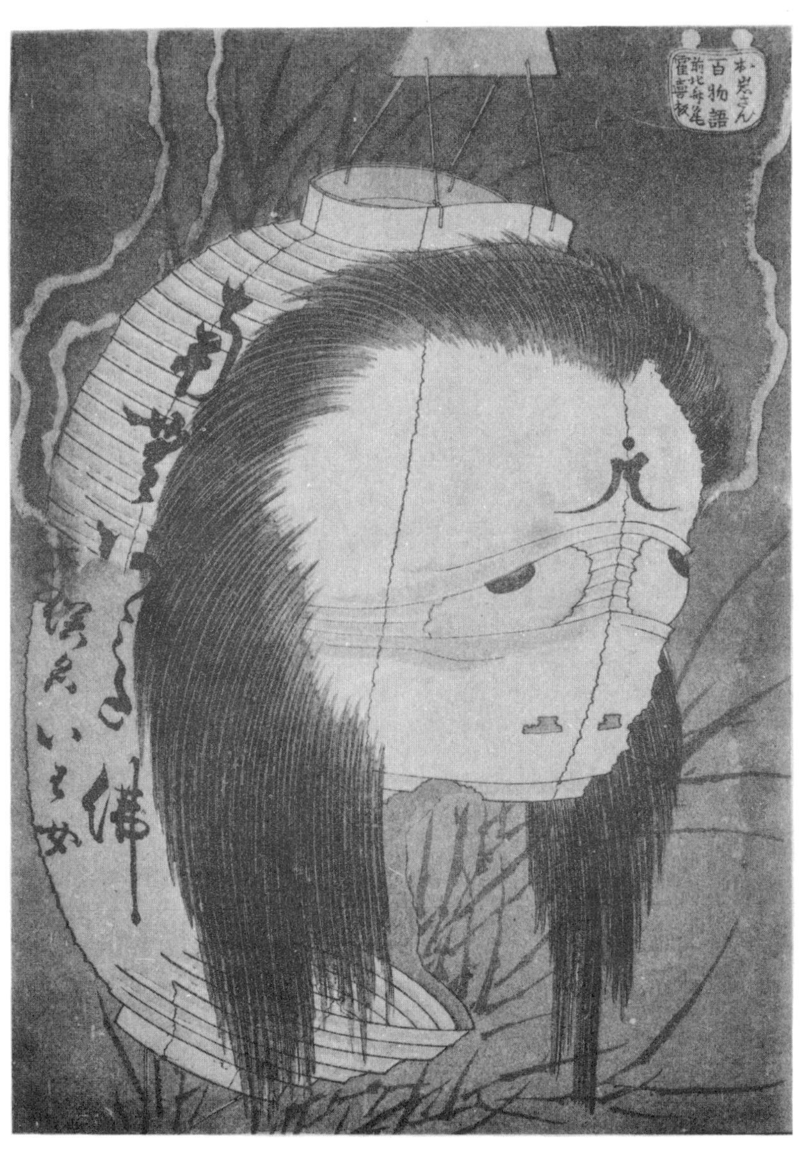
お岩さん
百物語
前北斎筆
鶴喜板

§14–18. Examples of Oiwa. Ghosts are evil, and their slightest influence spells doom for the unwary. Women ghosts are malignant, and they seek to destroy any living woman's happiness by casting wicked doubts on the faithfulness of loved ones, be they husbands or sweethearts.

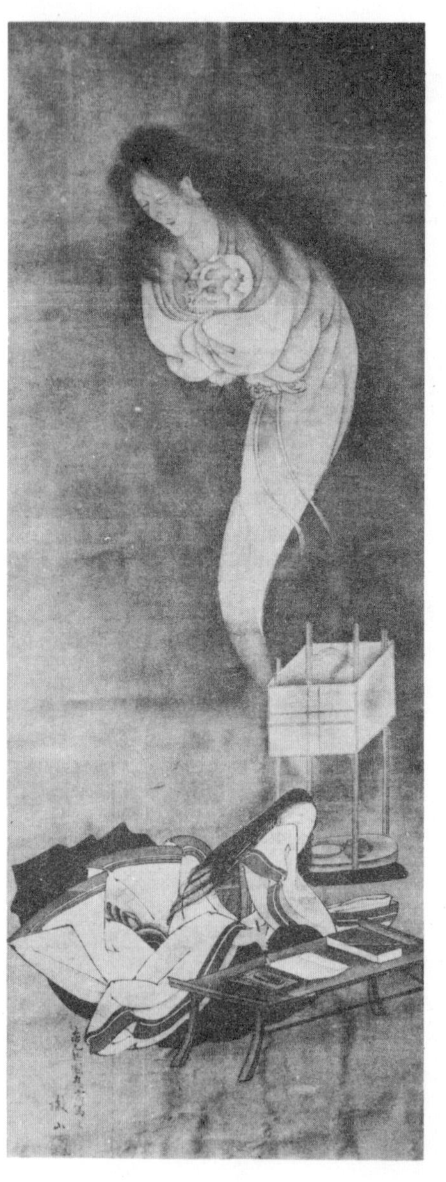

PART II

SUICIDE, MONSTERS, & FREAKS

§19. In Japan, men and women commit suicide in different ways. Men deem it honorable to hack through their bowels. Women consider it better to pierce their throats with a short knife. The results are messy and horrible to behold; so the sight of a woman suicide's ghost with her throat pierced and blood running from her mouth is particularly ghastly.

§20. A compounded folly is a double suicide, and such ghosts are especially pathetic. It is said that they haunt places lovers frequent and insidiously tempt the living into killing themselves. Instead of finding paradise with each other, the suicides find instead only horror and develop hate for each other. Hence their desire to take revenge on living lovers.

§21. Grasping the blade of a long sword, the man plunges it deep into his belly. Again and again, with superb courage, he bears the pain of the stabs and cuts as he kills himself. The red blood which spurts from the wounds looks black as it falls on the snow. His horror has just begun because his fate is fixed. He must return every year to the place of his death and as a ghost repeat his ghastly deed throughout the night. Ghost suicides are not logical, but neither are ghosts.

§22. Roads in old Japan were beset by demons. Lonely women traveling such roads were often attacked by creatures who made their appearances in a roll of thunder and smoke.

§23. While two priests doze, an evil demon comes to snatch a person away to hell. This is obviously a satire on the hypocrisy of many priests.

§24. Awaiting a visit from his lover, a dozing man is about to receive a rude awakening, for his visitor is no sweet simpering court lady but a long-tongued, repulsive demon who is about to tear him limb from limb. The lower picture shows the man driving this creature away with his sword.

公時

§25. A Nure Onna, or Wet Woman. In a diabolical manifestation, with long hair flying and tongue flickering to taste the wind, she is evil personified. Greatly feared by the fisher folk of northern Japan, she is to be avoided at all costs.

§26. The Wet Woman is seen during storms along the coasts of northern Japan. In this illustration she is clearly a snake with a female head.

§27. Demons are the voyeurs in the world of the weird. Fond of human women, they frequent their quarters after all is quiet to peek, leer, and giggle to themselves over sights such as unwary sleepers provide. They sometimes stealthily slip into a woman's bed and, without waking her, take their pleasure.

§28. With demons there is nothing that is sacred or that can be kept from their prying eyes. Here a demon puts aside a magic mallet, taking time out to peek into a room, no doubt in the hope of seeing something salacious.

§29. In Japanese art, humor and phallic symbolism abound. If an artist can combine ideas and symbols into one object, he feels he has achieved a special effect. Here a long-nosed demon is seen wrapped in a traditional carrying cloth, which rises up as the demon's nose assumes the form of an erect penis.

天狗の面を
風呂鋪に
包む

§30. The demon-gods Tengu are creatures man or woman should avoid. Tengu have the nasty reputation of seducing children and raping women or men. It is said that the very virtuous have nothing to fear from Tengu since, if they invoke his aid, he will help them. Tengu usually have a beak nose, but in this instance it is an elephant's trunk.

§31. Purity of heart and good intention are often served well by demons. This is a constant theme. Here a blind mendicant rests after a long, slow pilgrimage, while his two servants, both fearsome-looking Oni, wait upon their master with doglike (or, more exactly, demonlike) devotion.

役の小角
前鬼
後鬼

§32. The consolation of religion is offered a woman by a demon who impersonates a high-ranking Buddhist monk. She appears unperturbed by his terrible head.

柿本
貴僧正

§33. Demons have arguments as do human beings, and in this procession they go onward squabbling among themselves over some difference of opinion. This fascinating group is from the *Hokusai Manga*.

§34. Returning home, three brothers discover a drunken demon rollicking in their house. They are nonplused as to what to do. Should they call a priest and have the demon exorcised, throw the brute out themselves, or invite the monster to stay? The proper method of dealing with demons is not exactly known by this uncertain trio.

§35. When Buddhists die, they are laid out with their heads pointing south. If a living person sleeps with his head to the south, he is likely to be visited by a demon who will torment his sleep or even cause him to die.

○反枕
まくらがへし

§36. A glum monster sits and waits for his first victim of the day. Monsters frequently wait along the main roads of old Japan, and pity the poor victim who meets them! The many wayside shrines found throughout Japan were for wayfarers to pray for protection from demons.

§37. Hiding beneath a house ambulatory, a samurai keeps out of harm's way while two demons romp through his house spreading terror.

§38. Shunned, laughed at, and hated, leprous monsters are here cruelly treated by pilgrims, ignoring the priest who begs that they be helped.

§39. Made fearless by a night of grace and magic granted them once a year, inanimate objects and unearthly creatures pay mock homage to the lord of a mansion who, with perfect composure, accepts taunts and insults with patience.

§40. Common human beings cannot conquer demons. Heroes, saints, the virtuous, and inspired persons are the only people who can get the best of them. Chinese heroes, whom the Japanese greatly admired, were famous for defeating and conquering demons.

§41. Village trade is an everyday scene in Japan, but not by two such ghastly creatures with ghastly goods. A smaller demon hands an order to a larger demon for some delicacy, possibly for the human head and the fish carried in his tray.

§42. Prodigious in his appetite for both drink and women, a giant demon grasps a large bowl and a small woman.

§43. Demons do great mischief, yet if they can somehow be overcome they are required to become servant or slave to the subduer. Demons are stupid, yet they have many peculiar talents, one of these being the ancient art of cauterizing. Subdued by a Chinese hero, a demon applies this art to his master's back.

酒呑童子

§44. A sacred Buddhist dance is mocked by freaks and animals to the dismay of the miniature human beings at lower right, who obviously have no control over the situation.

§45. Every summer freaks, demons, witches, devils, animals, and animate objects make a pilgrimage to the mountains to attend the "hundred demons" festival. This is a caricature of the Japanese custom of making pilgrimages.

§46. Ghostly pilgrims with heads in the form of animals or demons make their way on an unearthly pilgrimage. Some have bird, cat, or monkey faces.

金

§47. If in the countryside at night the faint tolling of a bell is heard, it is not always the bell of an ordinary temple. The bell may be rung by a monster priest whose duty it is to toll it regularly. Many bells in Japan are famous for one reason or another. Some have been abandoned, except for their ghostly guardians.

§48. Deserted houses are shunned in Japan just as they are in the West. The Japanese believe that uninhabited houses are filled with ghostly freaks and monsters who take delight in frightening or doing worse things to human beings.

○野寺坊

天井下

§49. The Shokera, a spirit or monster of the rooftops, has the habit of spying on unsuspecting members of a household. Here one looks through a roof skylight.

§50. It is believed in Japan that the King of Freaks usually visits a household at six o'clock in the evening, and for that reason traditional Japanese are reluctant to go visiting at that hour.

○せうけら

○ぬらりひよん

§51. Fresh Japanese lacquer is volatile and if inhaled can cause dizziness, fainting, even death. The ancient Japanese believed that the spirit of the ancestral home shrine, which is usually highly lacquered, had an insidious effect upon the health.

§52. The Eyes-in-Hand Freak haunted reed plains. In ancient Japan the best trysting place for lovers was in the reed marshes, where they could meet privately. This particular freak seeks out such lovers and practices his unusual form of voyeurism.

○塗佛
ぬりぼとけ

○手の目

§53. The Human Dirt Freak severely punishes housewives. Unless a bath is kept scrupulously clean, this particular monster will collect all the human bath filth accumulated in a year and rub it on the offending housewife.

§54. This Stinking Monster is the spirit of the outhouse. It takes revenge on persons who have offended it by blowing faecal matter on them.

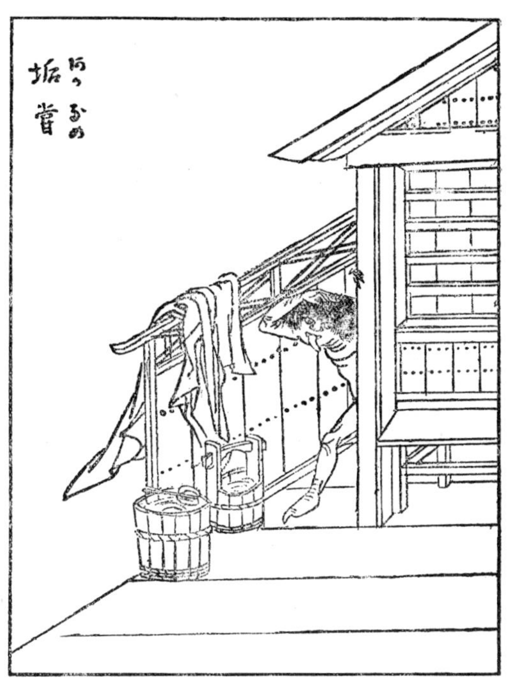
垢嘗

加牟波理入道

§55. In ancient Japanese belief every inanimate object has its protective guardian or spirit. This is one of the reasons that so many objects are worshiped in Japan. Here the spirit of a stone lantern makes its presence known by a threatening grimace.

§56. Along the wind- and sea-swept coasts of northern Japan, amongst the shore-driven seaweed and rubbish, is the woman called Nure Onna, or Wet Woman. With horrible features, long, slick, wet hair, and a body shaped like some sea snake, she inhabits the beaches, where she can eat offal.

古籠火

○濡女

§57. The water monster, or Kappa, is sometimes depicted as a jolly, greedy little elf, full of wholesome cuddliness. In old Japan Kappa were highly feared, especially for their nasty habit of grasping swimming children and drowning them for sport. There is a story which claims that Kappa could be bribed with cucumbers, but this tale must be of late origin, as Kappa were originally eaters of human flesh and drinkers of human blood.

§58. A demon tries to capture a wary Kappa by using a trap baited with a human body and set with a drawn bow and arrow.

○
河童 かつぱ

§59. The rainy season brings out the melancholy streak in the Japanese character. There is a story about a rain spirit who appears on roads in the evenings, or late in the afternoon, as a little misshapen boy. He is sometimes seen scurrying through the rain as if on an important mission, and he may stop before a house seeking directions. If the dweller is wise, he will not say a word to him, as it would bring bad luck to the household.

§60. One Japanese story has it that women are so fascinated with themselves and spend so much time gazing at mirrors because they are possessed by a demon spirit that lives in mirrors.

雨降小僧（あめふりこぞう）

雲外鏡（うんぐゎいきやう）

§61. The Eyeless Woman Monster frequents shrines and graveyards to entice men into amorous dalliance. She is to be avoided, since she is a lure set out by man-eating ghosts, and death, not sexual satisfaction, will follow any intimacy with her.

§62. This ghost of an Idiot Freak must wash red beans eternally because while alive it disobeyed a command of the magical white fox. It is condemned to this punishment until released from bondage by the Buddha's mercy.

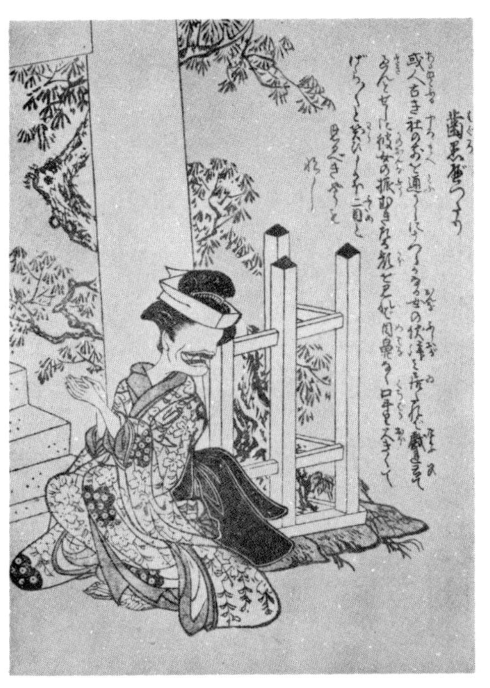
歯黒べつたり

小豆あらひ

§63. If one can obtain the services of the right witch or magician, it is possible to summon the spirit of a well, or a well monster guardian, which will then submit a list of names of persons who have committed suicide in the particular well.

§64. Japanese monsters are not attractive creatures and are least so when bent on mischief. Here a monster of a public bath bursts through the doors seeking to grasp some female victim and drag her away for rape or other purpose.

§65. The Japanese enjoy getting drunk, and sometimes they drink too much. However, being forced to get drunk is not pleasant. This samurai is seized by a drinking monster who insists that the samurai join him. This the man is reluctant to do, knowing that monsters, drunk or sober, are unreliable drinking companions.

§66. Wood is sacred in Japan; so before cutting a tree the woodcutter asks permission of a tree spirit. If the woodcutter happens to forget this courtesy, he is liable to be cut apart by the wood spirit, who uses as weapons (in this instance) the man's own tools.

§67. A demon priest serves as a mountain samurai's hairdresser. Demons, in the right circumstances, are excellent servants. This monster was probably bested in open combat and now serves his conqueror.

§68. Japanese heroes in the old days of Japan were true heroes. In later ages their deeds were exaggerated, to the extent that a man was transformed into superman. Here a mountain samurai of western Japan does battle with a primitive cannon against a winged creature that resembles a bow and arrow.

武田
玄信

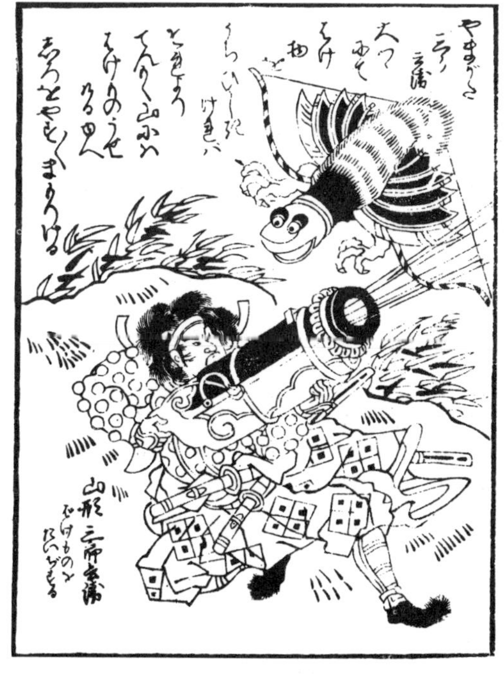
山形

§69. There is a Japanese belief that once a year inanimate objects come to life. During this time, it is their turn to dispense reward or punishment to the human beings they serve. Here a carpenter receives abuse from an old-fashioned line marker, an adze, and a log of wood.

§70. Screaming through the manor halls, rattling and moaning, thumping and blowing, a suit of armor, a war drum, and a shell war trumpet come to life to let their owner know that their time for seeking redress is upon him. In a brief spell of freedom these inanimate things express themselves, avenging wrongs done them in the course of the year.

§71. The Japanese have their own Walpurgis Night during the summer season, when there is a gathering of the monsters for the "hundred monsters" night festival. Inaminate objects become alive, animals assume human shape, and they join freaks and monsters to cavort, dance, and sing high in the mountains. During this unholy time, the Japanese shun certain mountain areas.

§72. These are monsters of the free Walpurgis Night as they are engaged in a "hundred monsters" festival.

百鬼夜行

§73. A tonsured monster who steals fire hides beneath the floors of Japanese houses. Ugly, secretive, and sneaky, this fire-licker is one of the better known house spirits.

火間蟲入道

§74. Making a meal of some hapless man, this two-tailed ghoul monster gnaws on a human leg just before washing it down with saké supplied from an animated saké barrel.

§75. Hiroshige, who loved bizarre, unusual, and magical subjects, took great paints to sketch them as he thought they should look. This magical white goat is now little known and of obscure history, but in Hiroshige's time it was deemed a good luck animal, most lucky if it had four sets of horns and five pairs of eyes.

白澤

§76. The Japanese are fascinated by freaks, and the greatest ever are depicted in the sketchbooks, or *Manga,* of the master woodblock artist Hokusai.

蛮国の
灸治

§77. This collection of strange creatures of basically human shape appears in the *Manga*.

飛頭蠻
穿胸
小人
狗国
三首
長脚
文身
柔利

§78. Recluses in Japan are often shabby, picturesque individuals who are called Yama-otoko, or Mountain Men. The average Japanese considered Yama-otoko somewhat uncivilized, often insane, and sometimes dangerous. Yama-otoko had strange companions such as she-wolves with human heads, monsters, freaks, and other creatures antagonistic to human beings.

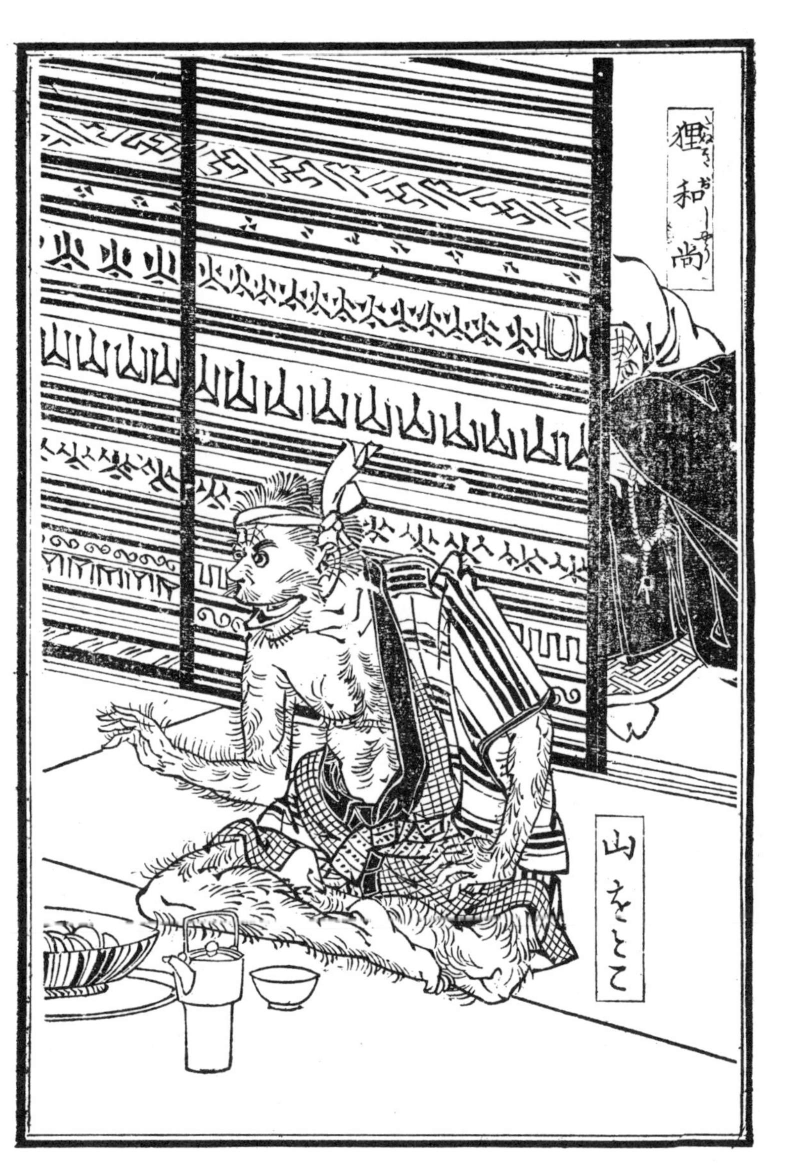
狸和尚
山をとこ

§79. The tea ceremony is a rather serious affair in Japan. Here this institution too is held up to ridicule and mockery by spirits, as a collection of outrageous freaks and monsters dressed in court finery prepare to go through the tea ritual.

§80. Girls who are inordinately fond of their good looks or their long hair may be visited by the Hair-Cutting Monster, or Kamikiri, who punishes their vanity by snipping off their locks.

かミきり

本書古法眼元信筆

阿部周防守正長写

§81. Japanese artists readily characterize animals, demons, and freaks as priests in holy acts, such as in the counting of beads in the "thousand-beads ceremony." The Japanese religious attitude is different from that of the West, making such ironic cartoons acceptable to even the most devout.

§82. Traditional Japanese have a healthy respect for demons, which they find fascinating, imagining them in all sorts of unusual situations. The demon-as-a-servant is a favorite theme. To draw an extremely ugly misshapen demon as the servant of these unwholesome-looking women is such an instance of fascination with the grotesque.

§83. Here a demon in the guise of a wandering mendicant strikes his wooden Buddhist clappers in a walking chant as he strolls past, accompanied by a woman with a dog's body.

§84. Nukekubi are unique long-necked creatures supposed to appear only when no one is about to see them. They are gentle and of benign temperament.

ぬけくひ

§85. As Nukekubi are not supposed to be seen, they can freely make their appearance before a blind man. Another blind man, with tremendous sang-froid, presents three-lens spectacles to a truly terrifying three-eyed monster.

§86. Nukekubi are usually females, either ugly or beautiful. All have necks which elongate and become snakelike in order to carry their heads floating around the room far from the bodies to which they remain attached.

§87. When this Nukekubi tells his tale, he frightens his one-eyed friend, who will not believe, since Nukekubi are said not to be seen. How can a one-eyed man see something that isn't there, even when two-eyed people can't see it? That seems to be the moral of this illustration.

○飛頭蛮
ろくろくび

長首

§88. Although traditionally not seen, Nukekubi are supposed to frighten people. This sumo wrestler, however, remains unperturbed and casually blows smoke in a three-eyed monster's face.

小野川喜三郎
月岡魁齋芳年

§89. In Japan there is a theory for everything, and one of these theories is about how gossip is spread. A ghost woman, two stories tall, overhears what is supposed to be private conversation, then passes along what she has heard to others.

§90. An old superstition claims that if a man adopts a daughter and deprives her of food, his own daughter, when born, will have two mouths and eat twice as much, as punishment to him for having deprived his stepdaughter of food. It is also believed that if a stepchild is murdered, any child born to its foster parents will have two mouths.

○二口女

§91. As man eater and baby eater, the female demon Hannya strikes terror in the heart of any person who meets her. In this instance a peasant stumbles across a man who has been transformed into a Hannya, and this frightens him out of his wits.

§92. Fire is feared in Japan for the most obvious reason, and the Japanese believe that if one steadily stares into a fire, one can see the demons contained in the flames. These spirits must be placated, tended to carefully, and never allowed to get out, lest they wreak damage by setting fire to the house.

§93. When candles are suddenly extinguished on a windless night, the Japanese attribute this to an old woman called Fukkeshi-baba, the Fire-Extinguishing Hag.

§94. Phallic-symbol freaks are often found in Japanese art. Depicted here is the god of longevity, with his high-domed head symbolizing a phallus, and another freak with a phallic nose.

ふつけし婆々

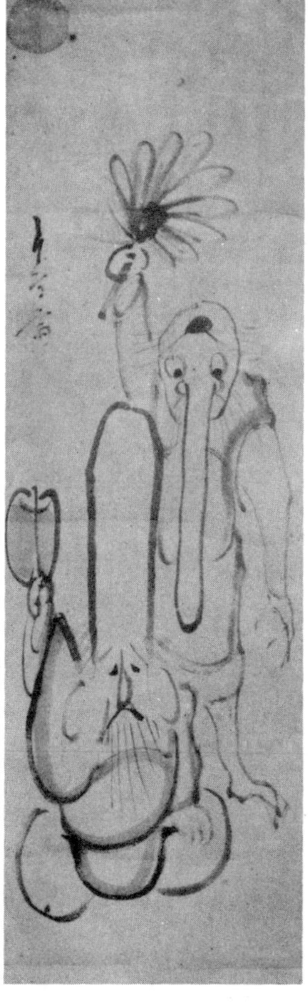

§95. Undaunted by the appearance of three visiting monsters, this classic Japanese hero bravely grasps his lacquered saké cup and stares his demon guests down.

§96. Hidden under the eaves of old temples are the strange creatures called Nupperabo. Although not sinister in any serious way, Nupperabo are uncomfortable things to meet. Their function, according to Japanese tradition, is to drive away impure persons from the confines of a temple.

§97. A painting of a Nupperabo showing its distinctively human, yet jellylike, face.

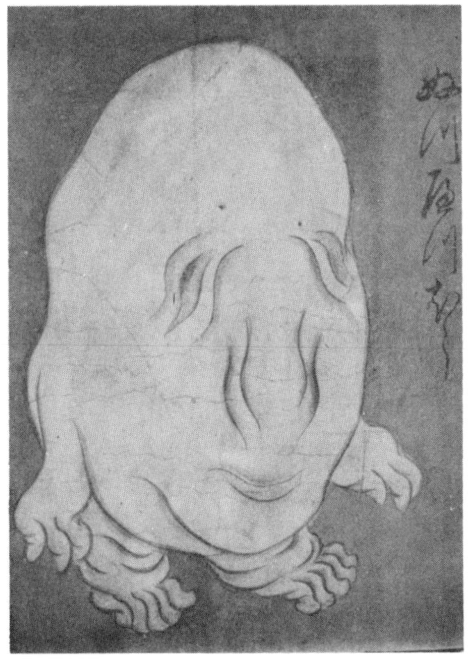

PART III

GHOULS & SKELETONS

§98. Ghouls fascinate the Japanese, who have taken a special delight in imagining them. To recognize a ghoul is not difficult, as it has insane, staring eyes, an unhealthy yet robust appetite, blood dripping from its mouth, and, often, blackened teeth.

§99. Here is Hannya, a true baby eater, the most feared demon in Japan. Hannya was a once beautiful woman who became mad and demoniacally possessed. In certain Noh plays, she is noted for cruelty toward young men. This is a rather unusual depiction of Hannya in the role of a ghoul. The artist has readily visualized her here as the ghastly eater who holds a baby's head, which she is about to devour.

笑ひはんにや
百物語
前北斎筆
鶴喜版

§100. A suicide victim has been dragged from a river, and her body is held to see if it will be claimed. An elegantly dressed gentleman arrives to say that he thinks the dead woman is his relative. Not wishing to offend anyone who is obviously so superior, the keeper of corpses permits the inquirer to examine the body alone, not realizing that his visitor is a demon ghoul in disguise, intent on eating the dead woman.

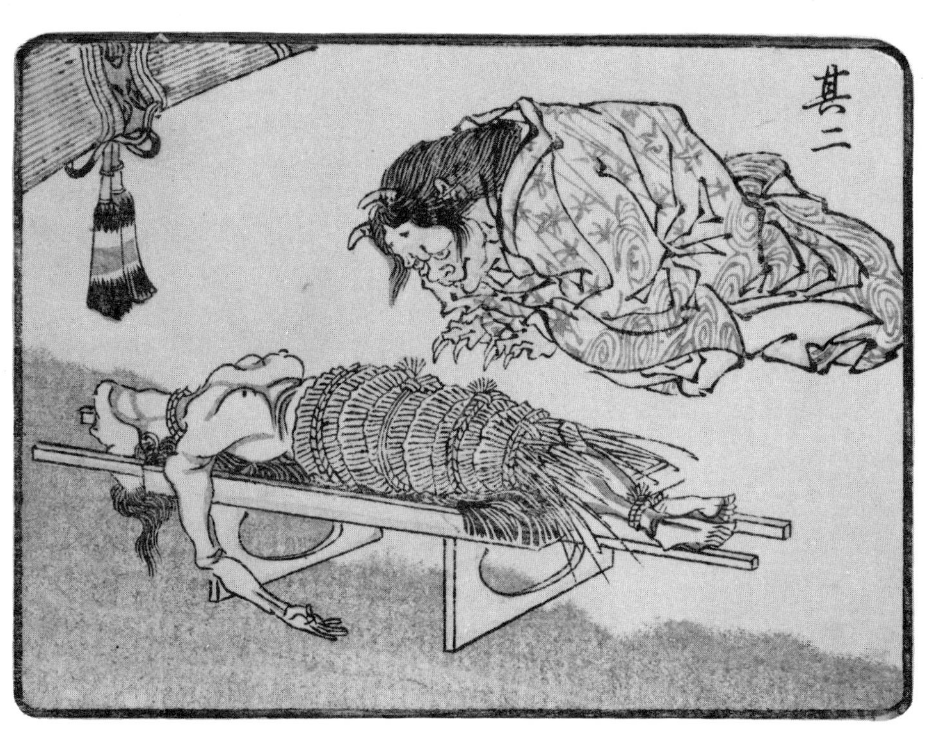
其二

§101. In part of old Japan, it was customary to leave the unclaimed dead at the section of the town wall known as the Tiger Gate. There the dead were at the mercy of the ghouls and ghosts who gathered to feast on corpses.

§102. Sometimes the unclaimed dead were grudgingly deposited in some local graveyard, where they were left to rot and where perverts, human monsters, and ghouls were free to forage among the bodies to satisfy every unhealthy appetite.

§103. The birth of a child to a ghoul family brought them joy, for there was a chance that the child would die and make it an occasion for feasting. This being the curious sentiment of domesticated ghoul demons, it is a wonder their race was perpetuated.

§104. The evil genius of a manor is here the symbolic skeleton of death. The lord of Shimoda foils an assassination attempt, and for the moment appears to have the situation well in hand. Yet it is only a question of time before death claims him too.

§105. This detail from the preceding illustration shows that the lord of Shimoda, successful in defending himself from man, has no defense against death, who peers at him in the form of a skeleton.

§106. A skeleton servant of a courtesan holds a lamp while she writes a letter to her lover. That the lover will never live to meet her may be surmised from the presence of this messenger of death.

§107. In Japan, typhoons often bring death to many; so a skeleton is their appropriate symbol. There is a Japanese saying that when a typhoon comes, death walks the land.

骸骨

§108. A symbol of retribution in Japan is the Buddhist wheel, which explains the expression, "the wheel comes full circle." It is said that at night, when man's conscience rests uneasily, with low rumbling the wheel of retribution slowly finds the sources of wickedness and evil and crushes them.

§109. The Japanese are very much aware of the incongruity of opposites. For effect, and to heighten horror, a skeleton slowly rises beneath a poetic new moon—the same moon that is such a constant theme in Japanese poetry of life, love, and beauty.

PART IV

MURDER

§110. On the old highway called the Kisokaido, a woman demon whose habit was to solicit men in order to lure them to their death meets her own death at the hands of a rugged samurai who slays her with a sickle.

木曾街道
六十九次之内
鵜沼
与右エ門
女房累

§111. The warrior Kiyomori, a great lord of Japanese history, slew hundreds of men in battle to survive unscathed. While still vigorous in his middle years, he retired to his country estate to live out the remainder of his days in peace. Here on a winter's night he is visited by snow-ghost skulls of men he has slain in his many battles.

雪月花
山城
六波羅雪
大政入道浄海

§112. Sakura Sogoro was crucified by his feudal lord when he dared to protest the heavy taxes imposed on the peasants of the fief. Here he appears as a messenger from hell with orders for the lord to prepare himself for death.

§113. Under the influence of a mirror ghost, the samurai Kyoemon attempts to murder his lover. The face of the ghost is that of a one-eyed female.

中村芝翫
かさね
岩井半四郎
五渡亭
貞虎画

§114. Torture slaying was practiced in old Japan. This detail shows a man so dying. The story is told in the following caption.

§115. Ghosts are considered bad under any circumstances, the female ghosts being the most malicious. Here a female ghost urges two men to kill a former lover who murdered her. The ghost of a man she has murdered herself appears on the scene and gloats over the demise of his rival in a curious combination of love, hate, and horror.

§116. Japan's most famous ghost story, *Yotsuya Kaidan,* has so many variations that it is at times difficult to believe that it is the same story. In one particular version the ghost of Oiwa, the murdered woman, returns to her faithless husband, who in a rage decapitates her. Gunze and Kaminasu, the companions of the husband, come under the ghost-wife's influence, and against their will they attempt to kill him.

尾上菊五郎
市川団十郎

§117. Crucified on the orders of his feudal lord, Sakura Sogoro returns to haunt him by suddenly appearing between the lord and his armrest. The pine tree on the screen in the background has also taken on a horrendous aspect.

一勇斎国芳画

PART V

HELLS & DEMONS

§118. Emma-sama is the King of Hell. In this particular quarter of Emma's kingdom the demons are ghouls who feed on sinners who have been traitors to their country, faithless to their spouses, or have in some way broken their trust. Hunted like animals, the sinners are caught, ritually slain, devoured, then brought to life to suffer again the same punishment in an endless torture.

§119. Demons of the Japanese hells are particularly vicious. Their work in hell is to harass the doomed, a duty in which they take delight. Foul, ugly brutes, these demons are the masters of hell. They have no mercy and revel in sadistic delight as they tear and burn their victims.

§120. The greedy have a special place in hell, particularly those who, while alive, fed themselves on the misery of other people. In hell they are bloated with hot and putrid blood, then beaten like drums by hell's demons. Seared by flame and tormented by Hitodama (Ghost Balls), the greedy are tortured for their misdeeds in the world.

§121. Torn apart with pincers, beaten to a pulp by clubs, burned by fire, and crushed by the Buddhist wheel of retribution—such is the fate of those who in life committed the sin of lying. The demons allow no rest or respite to dead liars.

§122. The extreme horror in Japanese hells is pictured with frightening effect. As believers in retribution and punishment for past sins, the Japanese have special hells for particular sins. Here the licentious are watched over by a hell demon as they feed on each other, in much the same way as they consumed their innocent victims in the real world.

§123. The usurious meet punishment by being whipped by flame and torn apart by their demon keepers. A Buddhist retribution wheel rolls over one victim who cries out in anguish and pain.

PART VI

MAGICAL ANIMALS

§124. The fox is the most feared and the most impudent creature in Japan. As a messenger of the gods, it is king of all animals. Here a white fox holds court wearing a skull as a crown. His attendants are a cat and a badger, also animals of superstitious dread.

§125. Shedding regal dignity, a white fox leads a shrew and a monkey in a mock Kabuki dance. The sly cunning of the fox, combined with his dignity as a supernatural medium of the gods, allows many roles for this creature in art and literature.

白狐之助
むじ内

§126. Surprising his wife as she is changing from woman to fox, a horrified husband discovers her true identity as she assumes her real form. Their child clutches its mother's nebulous robes as if to hold back this transformation.

妻籠
安倍保名
葛葉狐

§127. The fox-woman is prominent in Japanese erotic literature. One long story devoted to this theme is entitled *Fox Genji*. Discovered to be a fox after giving birth to a child, the fox-woman here takes one last look at her baby before returning to her animal form.

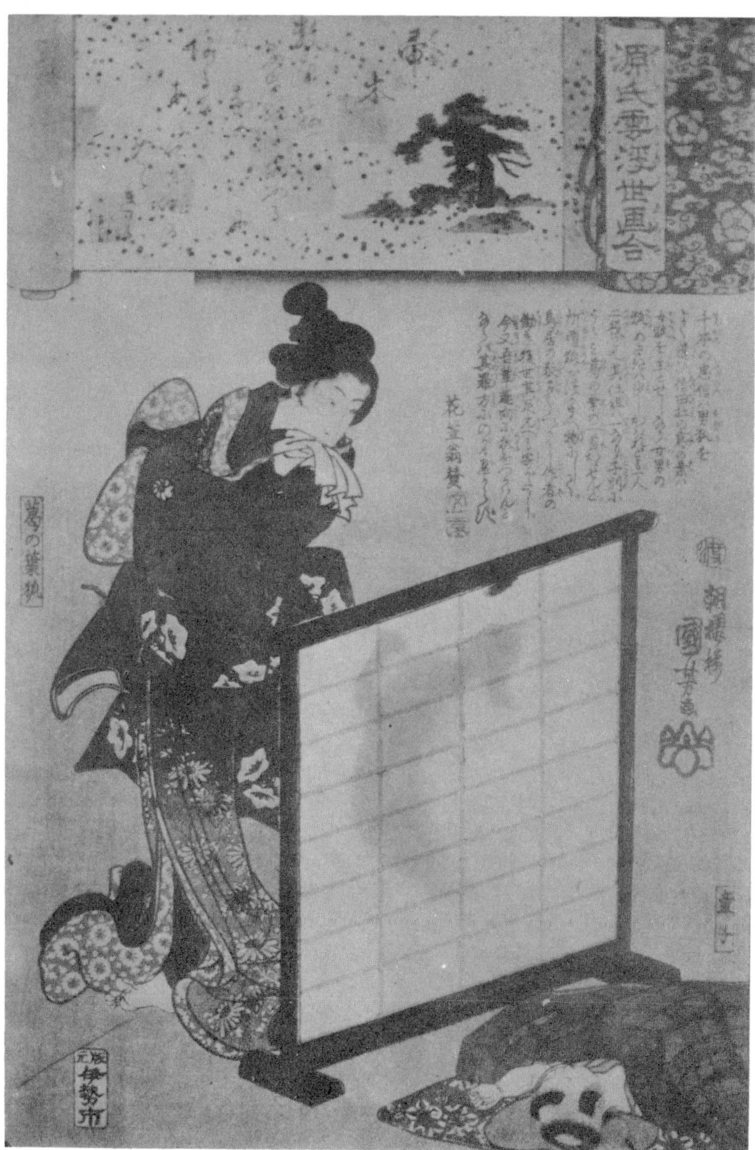
源氏雲浮世画合
葛の葉
花笠翁賛
朝櫻樓國芳画
板元 伊勢市

§128. In this illustration a fox-priest and his attendants and escort of cat-noble and other foxes or dogs make their way down the old Tokaido road. Some stories presented as fictional tales were bitter and fierce satires which, when recognized as such, often brought writer and illustrator to imprisonment and death.

§129. A gangster wolf-woman, dressed in magnificent robes and sitting in a fine room, accepts a bowl of saké. Her tricky nature is well caught by the artist.

§130. Here a group of elegantly dressed magical creatures catch a fox who has attempted to steal the three-eyed treasure of heaven. The penitent posture of the apprehended fox belies his true nature, which is deceptive and cunning.

社頭より兩
家の重寶
三眼の子息白狐之助
見越の息女轆轤姫
仝 執権青鷺の進

§131. In ancient days animals, especially foxes, were believed to dress in court garments and pretend to go on pilgrimages. Stopping along their route at the house of noblemen, they accepted food and lodging by utilizing, to their personal benefit, the obligation of courtesy to strangers.

§132. Foxes in the guise of noble travelers seek hospitality along the road. Two attendants carry lanterns while others support a palanquin.

§133. Here animal changelings celebrate a war feast with drinking and gaiety. The scene is a common one in Japanese myths and stories about fabulous creatures.

§134. Wolves believed to represent spirits of the mountains were reverenced by Japanese country folk. This devotion did not lessen the ferocity of the wolves, which ate their followers at every opportunity. Here a wolf walks off bearing the head of one of his devotees in its jaws.

狼

§135. In many Oriental cultures there is a firm belief that animals can inhabit human bodies. In Japan, as in the West, the cat is noted for its evil potential in this respect. Cats entered women's bodies to wreak havoc in a cruel and wanton manner.

§136. Cats are held sacred and are much feared because of their disposition to do evil. This clever picture is a composition of a number of cats which in turn form a single cat face.

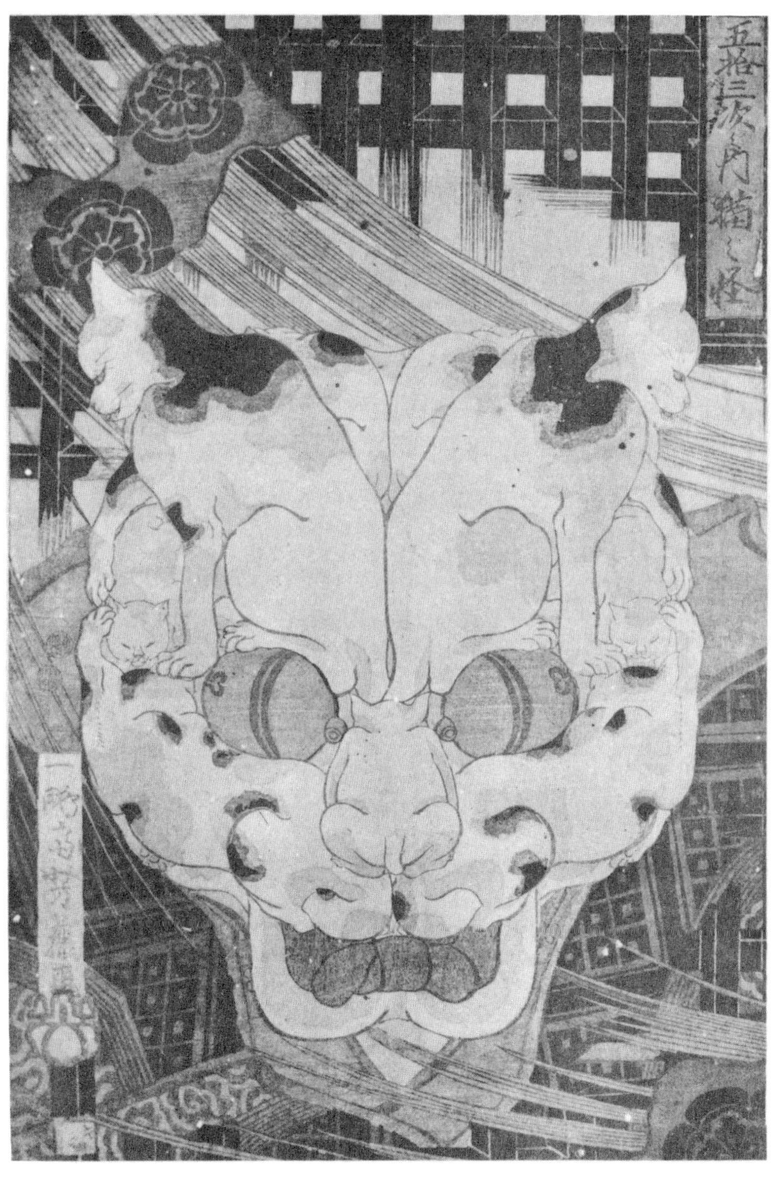
五拾三次之内猫之怪

§137. A cat in human form minces daintily by as two freaks prepare the curtains for a stage presentation. Here the animal has human arms and legs but a cat head.

§138. In this scene, an unholy love affair with a badger, who had assumed human form, obliges a woman to commit suicide in expiation of her shame. Her animal lover, in a suicide ritual, must cut off her head and then plunge the end of the sword into his own bowels.

見越の浪人狸
妻雪女郎

§139. Magical foes can be captured only by angels, according to Japanese tradition. Here an evil fox is being apprehended by a heavenly being who grasps its leg.

§140. A fox and a mountain man discuss some deed of mischief. Both are dressed in rich garments.

娘 姑獲鳥

山をとこ
たぬき

§141. A cat appears as a performer, watched by a fox and a one-eyed monster from the wings of the stage.

たぬき
狢内

PART VII

FABULOUS CREATURES

§142. Inhabiting the eaves or hidden places of a Japanese house is an animal known as an Amikiri, or Net Cutter. It delights in mischief of any kind.

§143. The bird called Tommoraki is a harassing messenger of evil forces. When Buddhist priests recite ritual chants, the Tommoraki vomits and screams obscenities in its attempts to prevent the chants from being effective.

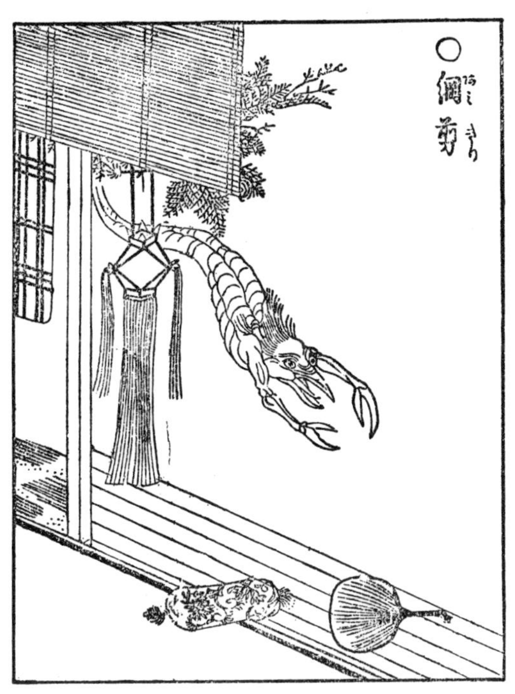
○網剪（あみきり）

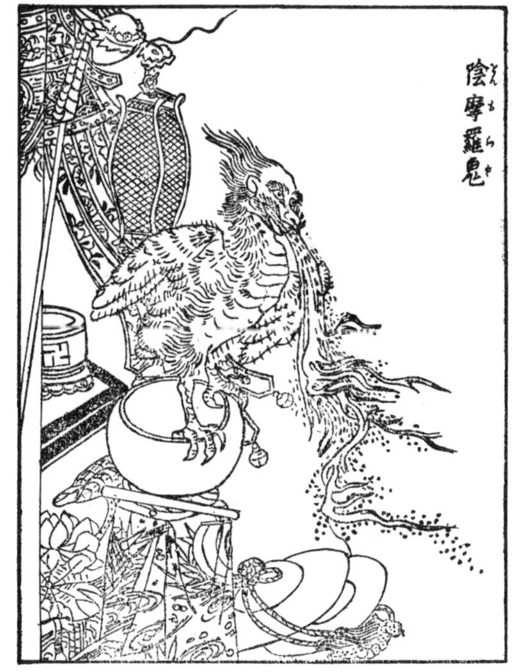
陰摩羅鬼（をんもらき）

§144. It is believed in certain rural areas of Japan that gossips are sometimes transformed into red-tongued monsters condemned to haunt crossroads.

§145. Lurking on quiet out-of-the-way roads is a beast known as a Waira, which preys on unsuspecting children.

○赤舌
あかした

○をいら

§146. A spider demon snatches at the head of an unsuspecting man. Such monsters were firmly believed in by the people of old Japan, but today they are merely part of an interesting tradition.

§147. The animal named Otoroshi had the duty to protect temples and shrines from being visited by impious persons. When such a person entered sacred grounds, an Otoroshi pounced on him with shrill screams and tore the offender to pieces.

○おとろし

§148. Here a giant toad hops into a garden from a house, knocking over a lamp and a sliding paper door. Its shape is that of a natural toad; however, its gigantic size indicates that it is a supernatural creature.

§149. This young girl discovers that she is really a frog in human form. As a child she was transformed into a human being and brought up by human stepparents. Now, however, she must return to her own kind.

§150. The Joro Kumo, or Courtesan Spider, is appropriately symbolical. The Japanese see in a prostitute the nature of a spider, and the illustrator, by giving free rein to imagination, has come up with the fascinating hybrid of spider and woman.

§151. Martens are thought to haunt old houses by descending from the heavens at night, using their own bodies to make ropes to earth. They return to heaven in the same manner after their tasks on earth are done.

○
絡新婦
ぢよらうぐも

○
鼬
てん

§152. Caught in the rolled coils of a supernatural snake monster, a woman is slowly crushed to death while her lover prudently runs away to save his own life.

§153. The mountain hero Jinta Shiro, famed in song and legends, is here seen slaying a giant mountain shrew, a creature believed to be triple-sexed. In the lower illustration a devilish creature torments a man with rope and rod.

仁田四郎
瓜盗人

§154. The hero Sanjuro battles a giant spider of fearsome aspect. Enlarged insect monsters have inspired terror in many cultures, but they become their most monstrous in Japanese art.

國長画

§155. The two fighting Tengu are among the best of Japanese grotesqueries. No one knows from what unholy egg they were hatched, but we can be sure they are not of this earth. The illustration is from the *Hokusai Manga*.